I0053296

—Live Your—
Big Dream

A Step By Step Plan

H. RICHARD STEINHOFF

Live Your Big Dream: A Step-by-Step Plan © 2018 H. Richard Steinhoff. All rights reserved.

No part of this publication may be reproduced or transmitted in any form or by any means, chemical or electronic, including photocopying and recording, or by any information storage and retrieval system, without permission in writing from Author or Publisher (except by a reviewer, who may quote brief passages and/or show brief video clips in a review.)

Disclaimer: The Publisher and the Author make no representations and warranties with respect to the accuracy or completeness of the contents of this work and specifically disclaim all warranties, including without limitation warranties of fitness for a particular purpose. No warranty may be created or extended by sales or promotional materials. The advice and strategies contained herein may not be suitable for every situation. This work is sold with the understanding that the Author and Publisher are not engaged in rendering legal, coaching, psychological, accounting, or other professional services. If professional assistance is required, the services of a competent professional person should be sought. Neither the Publisher nor the Author shall be liable for damages arising herefrom. The fact that an organization or website is referred to in this work as a citation and/or a potential source of further information does not mean that the Author or the Publisher endorses the information the organization or website may provide or recommendations it may make. Further, readers should be aware that Internet websites listed in this work may have changed or disappeared between the time this work was written and when it was read.

Some names and identifying details have been changed and some of the story lines have been recreated.

Praise for
Live Your Big Dream:
A Step-by Step Plan

"Richard Steinhoff has made it possible for anyone to navigate the complicated world of real estate investing. Reading this book will help everyone, from the weekend investor to the sophisticated developer, avoid costly errors. This book is a must read for anyone thinking of buying real estate, whether they plan to use it as their primary residence or as an investment property."

—Dr. Dilip Tapadiya

"*Live Your Big Dream: A Step-by Step Plan*" is certainly a must read for every new investor considering any type of real estate investment as well as investors who have not thought about real estate before but probably should have. There is a lot of real estate wisdom and experience expressed in a concise guide. This is a great resource for anyone looking for a realistic way to finance their Big Dream."

—Robert W. Smith,
President, Sage Community Group, Inc.

"Richard Steinhoff gives the new real estate investor an easy to follow plan together with definitions of the terms used in real estate transactions. You will learn the essential points of being a successful real estate investor by reading this book. This is a must-read before you start looking for an investment!"

—Marc Goldin,
CFO, The Crean Foundation

"Richard Steinhoff has done it again with his new book, *Live Your Big Dream*. He cuts to the chase by explaining only the steps you need to know (Brass Tacks) to choose and purchase an investment property. An easy read, plus learning the calculations and differences between the various types of income properties and cost comparisons gives me confidence to go out and live my dream."

—Kristine Weatherly,
CFO Spectrum Mechanical

"H. Richard Steinhoff has created an excellent introduction to commercial real estate investing. Written in easy to understand language and augmented with the real life client stories, this publication provides the reader with a simple, 7 step process of entering into the commercial real estate investment world. As a perspective commercial real estate investor, I found this very helpful."

—Brian Fredette,
Prospective Real Estate Investor

"This is a great primer covering all the basics. It discusses the major asset classes with the pluses and pitfalls to watch for in each. Excellent resource for investors."

—Larry W. Heglar,
MAI, Appraisal Institute

ACKNOWLEDGEMENTS

I WANT TO THANK JOHN McDERMOTT for your great insight and valuable advice. You are always right there for me when I need you.

Thanks to Brian Fredette for your beneficial suggestions about the content.

I want to thank my entire family for your constant support and encouragement. Thank you Elaine, Lisa, Brian, Sydney, Rick, Mary Anne, Brittany, Chris, Michael, Ryan, Jasmine, Nina, Kevin, Cameron, Tonia, Hailey, Hannah, Josue, Debbie, Jerry, Kaitlyn, and Diana.

Thanks to Larry Heglar, Kristine Weatherly, Marc Goldin, Brian Fredette, Robert Smith and Dr. Dilip Tapadiya for providing endorsements. You are all truly special to me.

FOREWORD

ONE OF MY FAVORITE CLOTHING lines for casual wear is "Life is Good". I bought one of their earliest baseball caps when they first began their epic growth to popularity and embroidered on the inside of that hat is their motto; "Do what you Like; Like what you do". Is there anything better than that as a dream for our lives?

Rich Steinhoff is exactly that guy...doing what he likes and loving what he does...bringing nuggets of real estate investment knowledge to all of us. Simply, passionately and from experience, he wants all of his readers to enjoy some level of financial independence that only commercial real estate can provide by creating passive income and ultimately, wealth.

In his new book," *Live Your Big Dream*," Richard provides a wealth of information from his own experience to give you a strong understanding of how real estate investing can actually provide the income needed for you to pursue your Big Dream,

If you are looking for a way to fund your Big Dream, this book can help make it happen for you. I highly recommend you invest in it, learn all you can and utilize the information inside to provide a road map for you to help assure your success.

-- John McDermott,
Executive Director, SVN Chicago Commercial

CONTENTS

INTRODUCTION

ARE YOU EXCITED ABOUT WHAT you do? Do you experience joy every day? Do you wake up and can't wait to get started with your day? If not, you are living Off-Purpose. You really don't want to be there because you will never be happy and life will feel like a struggle.

You should give this some thought. How would your life change if you did not have to be concerned about money and you could live your Big Dream? If you read my book," Dying On Purpose," you would know that doing what you love would not only benefit others but would also allow you to live a joyous, fulfilling life. But you need residual income to make it happen. For most people, the way to do it is by investing. You have to leverage your money. You can't make it by working for a salary. 70% of all Americans live paycheck-to-paycheck.

When you are considering investing, the two best choices are the stock market or real estate. Within real estate investments is a category called Real Estate Investment Trusts (REIT). They are traded on the stock market exchange. A REIT buys and operates real estate income producing property, like apartments, retail centers, office buildings, single tenant net leased properties, and hotels. They pay dividends directly to their shareholders.

Here are the issues with REIT's:

1. They can be hurt by rising interest rates.
2. The dividends you receive are taxed at ordinary income rates.
3. Their income fluctuates due to a number of factors.
4. They are subject to the volatility of the real estate market.
5. You have no control over management of your assets.
6. Most REIT's have only one asset class, so they are subject to the market fluctuation of that class.

Some financial advisers recommend staying away from REIT"s completely because they believe the potential downside is too great or the market value if the REIT (stock) is greater than the value of the assets the REIT owns. Therefore, we will initially eliminate REITs in our plan.

Here are the differences between stocks and real estate investments:

1. Real estate is real property. Everything else will come and go but real property will always be there. You can pass it down from generation to generation. It is also often lower in risk.
2. Stocks are not a tangible asset. You own a piece of paper. It also has a higher risk potential.
3. Real estate is less liquid and has a higher transaction cost than stocks.
4. According to the National Association of Realtors, real estate has had an average annual appreciation rate of 6.34% over the last 50 years.
5. According to the NYSE, stocks annual appreciation was 9.05% over the same period. However, Warren Buffet

said you shouldn't count on more than a 6-7% return over time.

6. Real estate's biggest advantage is leverage. For example, a $100,000 investment in the stock market will produce an annual return of $9,000 using the 50 year average.

The same $100,000 invested in real estate would allow you to purchase a $400,000 property. With an annual appreciation rate of 6.34% on the $400,000, the gain would be $25,000. In addition, you have an annual net rental income of $24,000 at a cap rate of 6%. Your total annual return would be $49,000. To obtain your net return, you have to subtract the loan payment of $18,000, giving you a net return of $31,000, vs the $9,000 in stocks.

(Note: All numbers throughout the book have been rounded off for ease of reading.)

So What Should You Invest In?

- You should consider investing in stocks if you don't have a lot of money and you need it to be liquid.
- You should consider investing in real estate if you want higher return on your money and you don't need it to be liquid.

Here are some reasons to buy investment real estate:

1. **Historically low interest rates**- current rates are the lowest in years. It makes buying investment property much more attractive.
2. **Return on investment**- conservative investments like money market accounts currently have a very low rate

of return, while investment properties produce 6-7% return.

3. **IRS 1031 Exchange**- this allows you to trade up to a higher priced property and defer paying capital gains. This alone should temp you to invest.

4. **Rising rental rates**- current investment property rental rates are rising faster than any recent period.

5. **Appreciation**- as previously stated, real estate appreciates at an average of about 6% per year. This increases your equity and your net worth.

6. **Income**- your investment will provide positive cash flow for you to use anyway you like. We will show you a great way to do that later in the book.

Just so you know, 70% of all wealth in America is in real estate.

It is not my intention to present you with a complete reference manual on how to become an expert investor. There are countless books on that subject. Instead, I will provide you with an overview of the process so that you are at least armed before going into battle.

Keep in mind, this is not a get rich quick plan, but it is a plan that will create the residual income you need to pursue your Big Dream.

To your success,
H. Richard Steinhoff
http://www.hrichardsteinhoff.com

Learn the Basics

BUYING AN INVESTMENT PROPERTY CAN provide the monthly income you need to fund your Big Dream. However, you do need a certain level of knowledge to become an effective investor. Learn everything you can, including the terminology, before you get involved in investing.

Investment Types

The worst investment is one unit, the next worst is two units, and so on. The reason for that is the return on investment and the risk. If you have four units and one is vacant, you still have income from the other three units. But if you have a house (one unit) and it is vacant, you have no income. Also, the income from four units will be proportionately higher than one unit—a house—which will give you better cash flow.

A lot of commercial properties are rented on a triple net (NNN) basis, which means the tenant pays the property taxes, insurance, and maintenance costs. That also makes for easier management.

The following is a summary of the core investment property types:

1. **APARTMENTS:**

   Disadvantages: Can be expensive to maintain.

   - Typically management-intensive. The magic number is 20 units, when it becomes economically feasible to hire a full-time resident manager
   - Rehab or turnover costs when tenants move out can be significant.

   Advantages: People always need a place to live, so you have fewer vacancies.

   - Easier to finance. If you buy two to four units, and live in one, you can often obtain favorable owner-occupied financing. Depending on price, you may be able to obtain a low down payment FHA loan on a 2-4 unit building if you occupy one unit.

2. **INDUSTRIAL** – Often a tilt-up concrete warehouse building with some office space. Can be single-tenant or multi-tenant.

   Disadvantages: Single-tenant buildings are more risky.

   - Difficult to rent if the building was modified to suit a particular tenant.

Advantages: Leases are generally modified gross, so you can pass expenses on to the tenant.

- The most stable of all property types (lowest price per square foot of all products.)
- Least management-intensive of all property types. You can basically lease it and forget it

3. **OFFICE** – Fully improved building with drop ceilings, heating and air-conditioning, private offices, and lobbies. Can be single-tenant or multi-tenant. Recently a growing trend has emerged: office condominiums. However, these are usually owner-occupied.

Disadvantages: Often difficult to lease. Typically has the highest vacancy rate of any property type.

- Single-tenant buildings are more risky
- More difficult to finance
- Landlord usually pays expenses

Advantages: The exception is the medical office building, which is easier to rent if well located and financing is usually accessable.

4. **RETAIL** – Can be a single-tenant building (like a restaurant) or a multi-tenant building (like a neighborhood shopping center).

Disadvantages: Difficult to keep rented in bad economic times.

- Need to spend money to maintain exterior appearance

Advantages: Leases are NNN, tenant pays expenses. (except roof and structure.)

- Less management-intensive than offices or apartments

There are also **MIXED-USE** projects, a combination of office and retail, or apartment and retail, which turn out to be more challenging to underwrite and manage.

And then there is **LAND**, which usually generates no income and is considered an "alligator" because you have to keep feeding it. This is generally not good for most people, especially first-time investors, because you have nothing but negative cash flow.

Some people say that land is good if you keep it for the long term.

If you believe that, look what happened to land between 2009 and 2010. Land prices went down more than 80 percent. You couldn't give it away. In some cases, residential land values were less than zero, because the falling house prices wouldn't even support a land acquisition price of zero! Even if the builders could get the land for free, they would still lose money. Also, you can't depreciate land.

Real Life Investor

Paul was a very intelligent man. As a matter of fact, he was a member of the American Mensa Society. He came to our office one day looking to buy an investment property. We matched him with our agent Mark, who was an experienced investment broker.

Mark was quite familiar with lender requirements for investment buyers, so he sat down with Paul to find out his investment goals. Paul had a very high six-figure income and $300,000 for a down payment.

Mark explained the different types of investment property:

- Apartments
- Industrial
- Office
- Retail

He told Paul about the advantages and disadvantages of each. After finishing, he asked Paul which he would prefer, and Paul told him he wanted to buy a single-family house.

Mark was startled. He asked Paul if he had not been listening to what he'd just said.

Paul assured him he had, but he still insisted on buying a house.

Mark said, "If I can show you that it makes more sense to buy a commercial property, will you at least consider it? Paul said he would.

Mark began explaining the difference between commercial and residential income properties. Using the example outlined in Figure 7.1, he showed Paul the differences in cash flow between single family, apartment, and industrial properties.

Apartments provided $21,000 more net income than single family, and industrial provided $36,000 more. Also, the industrial property lease was modified gross, which means you can pass expenses on to the tenant.

Mark then asked Paul what he now thought about buying a single family house. Paul hesitated a moment, then asked, "What do you have in industrial property?"

After looking at several industrial properties, Paul used his $300,000 to purchase a multi-tenant industrial building at a 7.4 percent cap rate, which provided him a positive cash flow of $19,000. He was a happy camper.

Figure 7.1:   Sample Investment Property Comparison

	Single Family	Apartment	Industrial
Purchase Price	$1,000,000	$1,000,000	$1,000,000
Down Payment	250,000	300,000	350,000
Loan Amount	$ 750,000	$ 700,000	$ 650,000
Loan Payment	[1] 48,000	[2] 45,000	[3] 42,000
Interest Rate	5%	5%	5%
Income	60,000	80,000	75,000
Expenses	18,000	20,000	3,000
Net Operating Income	42,000	60,000	72,000
Cap Rate	4.2%	6.0%	7.2%
Net Operating Income	$ 42,000	$ 60,000	$ 72,000
Loan Payment	48,000	45,000	42,000
Cash Flow Before Taxes	($ 6,000)	$ 15,000	$ 30,000
Cash Flow	($ 6,000)	$ 15,000	$ 30,000
Divided by Down Pmt.	250,000	300,000	350,000
Cash-on Cash Return	(3%)	5%	8.5%

---

[1]   Loan payment based on a $750,000 loan at 5% interest, amortized over 30 years

[2]   Loan payment based on a $700,000 loan at 5% interest, amortized over 30 years

[3]   Loan payment based on a $650,000 loan at 5% interest, amortized over 30 years

Financing

Lenders evaluate income properties using a debt coverage ratio. That ratio is calculated by dividing the net operating income by the proposed loan payment. In Figure 7.1, the debt coverage ratio for apartments would be 1.3 ($60,000 divided by $45,000) and the ratio for industrial would be 1.7 ($72,000 divided by $42,000).

The current debt coverage ratio being used for qualification by many lenders is around 1.25. Lenders are more comfortable with this because there is a 25 percent cushion for unforeseen problems, such as vacancies or emergency repairs. (Net operating income is 125% of the annual debt service.)

If you want to buy investment property, don't let the fear of financing hold you back if you have good credit.

Terminology

If you are going to play the game, you need to know the terminology. When people talk to you about cap rates, gross rate multiplier, or debt-to- income ratio, and they get your blank stare, it's not a good sign. You could be in a lot of trouble as an investor. You need to know what all the numbers mean, so here is a quick tutorial on important investment terms.

Capitalization Rate (Cap Rate): The percentage of return on investment used to determine the value of income property through capitalization. The cap rate is determined by dividing the Net Operating Income (NOI) by the property price expressed as a percentage.

To illustrate, using the data from Figure 7.1, dividing the net operating income for industrial of $72,000 by the sales price of $1,000,000, gives you a cap rate of 7.2 percent.

$$\text{Cap Rate} = \frac{\text{Net Operating Income}}{\text{Sales Price}} \quad \frac{\$72,000}{\$1,000,000} = 7.2\%$$

The cap rate is the most widely used number for comparing value when buying investment property. The higher the cap rate, the riskier it is for the investor. Lower cap rates are lower risk.

Gross Rate Multiplier: calculated by dividing the price by the gross income. In the above example, dividing the price of $1,000,000 by the gross income of $75,000 would create a GRM of 13.3. Sellers want that number to be high; buyers want it to be low. It's not a reliable indicator of value because it doesn't take into account the property expenses, which can vary widely. But it can tell you whether the price is in the ballpark.

$$\text{Gross Rate Multiplier} = \frac{\text{Sales Price}}{\text{Gross Income}} \quad \frac{\$1,000,000}{\$75,000} = 13.3$$

Gross Income: The total income of the property. In Figure 7.1, it is $75,000.

Net Operating Income (NOI): Total income less all expenses, other than mortgage payments. Again, using Figure 7.1.

Net Operating Income= Gross Income $75,000 – Expenses $3,000 = $72,000

Debt to-Income Ratio: This number is used by banks to determine how much money to lend on a property. The number is derived by dividing the net income of the property by the loan payment. Using the above example, the annual loan payment would be $42,000 and the net operating income is $72,000. Dividing $72,000 by $42,000 gives you a debt-to-income ratio of 1.7.

$$\text{Debt-to-income-ratio} = \frac{\text{Net Operating Income} \quad \$72,000}{\text{Loan Payment} \qquad \$42,000} = 1.7$$

Pro Forma Income: Projected income of an investment property is usually based on full occupancy and market rents, not actual income.

Cash-on Cash Return: Net operating income less loan payment, divided by down payment, expressed as a percentage. Using Figure 7.1, dividing $30,000 cash flow for industrial by $350,000 down payment gives you a 8.5% cash-on-cash return.

$$\text{Cash-on-cash} = \frac{\text{Cash Flow} \quad \$30,000}{\text{Down Payment} \quad \$350,000} = 8.5\%$$

Review this chapter frequently to keep your knowledge current.

Assemble Your Team

I F YOU'RE GOING TO BE a successful investor, you will need a good team with to work with. The team should consist of resources in all of these areas:

- Commercial real estate broker
- Commercial lender
- Property inspector
- Building contractor
- Property manager
- Real estate attorney
- CPA

This may seem like a daunting task, but it isn't as hard as you might think.

First, you start by finding a good, competent commercial investment broker. This will make the whole investment experience user-friendly and remove a lot of the stress, particularly since they can introduce you to the other team resources.

The best way to select a good broker is the same way you select a doctor, dentist, or hair stylist. You get a referral!

People have received good broker referrals from their insurance agents, their financial advisors, their attorneys, and their stockbrokers. Someone you know will surely have had a good experience with a commercial real estate broker. This way, you have the opportunity to work with a broker who has a good track record with an acquaintance, and who wants to maintain a good reputation by taking great care of you. In addition to the commission, the agent's incentive is to do well so that he will receive more referrals from your friends—and maybe even from you!

Your commercial broker can then assist you in finding a commercial lender, property inspector, building contractor, property manager and real estate attorney. You probably already have a CPA or tax accountant. You can also ask your friends, your neighbors, your relatives, your co-workers, and your service providers for a referral.

Now that you have your team in place, you are ready for step 3.

Develop a Plan

WORK WITH YOUR INVESTMENT BROKER to create a long-term investment plan.

Your plan should include:

- How much money you want to invest
- How much debt you want to take on
- Type or types of property you want to buy
- Location of the property
- Timing of your investment
- Purchase price of the property.
- Pre-approval letter from lender

If you want to get a feel for the process before you jump in full force, you can start with a small investment like a duplex or fourplex. Here's an example of a first-time investors experience.

First Time Investor

Gordon and Sue had been in their home for a while, and had managed to save $50,000. They both worked and had a significant income. Their tax advisor suggested they consider buying an investment property to help offset their large tax bill, so they contacted our agent, Janet, who had sold them their house.

Janet was also experienced in small investment properties. The first thing she did was talk with a commercial lender about Gordon and Sue's qualifications, so she knew what she had to work with. The lender told her that they would probably qualify for a property around $200,000, depending on property type and income.

Commercial loans are primarily based on the property, but lenders also want the buyer to have sufficient resources to cover unforeseen expenses. Janet then scheduled an appointment to meet with Gordon and Sue.

After they arrived, Sue said, "Isn't it difficult to buy investment property?"

Janet told them that people do it every day, and the key was to start small. She recommended starting with a duplex (a two-unit apartment building). She also told them about talking with the lender, and that they would be able to buy in the $200,000 range.

Janet said she would be holding their hand throughout the entire process, and then explained how it works. She showed them how they could use the interest on the loan, property tax, insurance, and maintenance as a write-off against the income.

They could also depreciate the building portion of the property as an additional deduction. Janet illustrated this by using the example shown in Figure 7.2. Here, they would have an annual positive cash flow of $1,600 ($16,800 income less $15,200 loan payment and expenses). They would also have a $2,600 write-off against ordinary income on their tax returns. Not huge numbers, but a great start in the world of investment.

The best part was, with the tenants rent essentially covering the mortgage and expenses, Gordon and Sue would be building equity in the property without actually paying for it. (Welcome to my world!)

The same principle can work for you based on your individual numbers.

This will create a magical situation for you as an investor, which is detailed in step seven

> **TIP: When buying an investment property, always use an experienced broker.**

Figure 7.2: Income Property Analysis Example

Purchase Price:	$200,000
Down Payments	<u>50,000</u>
Loan Amount	$150,000
Gross Income	$ 16,800
Expenses:	
Property Tax	$ 2,400
Insurance	800
Maintenance	<u>1,200</u>
Total	$ 4,400
New Operating Income	$ 12,400
Loan Payments	<u>10,800</u>
Cash Flow	$ 1,600
For taxes:	
Income $16,800	
Less expense	4,400
Less interest	9,500
Less depreciation	5,500
Gain/ (Loss)	($ 2,600)

STEP 4

Evaluate Properties

N OW THAT YOU HAVE A plan, you broker can select available properties for you to evaluate. I always recommend meeting with your broker first to go over the numbers. You'll probably eliminate some properties right away so that you don't have to waste time looking at them.

Then you can drive by the properties that look good on paper to check them out. Remember, you will most likely not be able to view the inside of the property because the owners will not want to continually disturb their tenants. Your offer will be subject to an interior inspection of the property.

Here are some tips to help with your evaluation:

1. Extra amenities/swimming pools

Typically, swimming pools are found in apartment buildings, which are already high maintenance. The last thing you want, particularly if you are a first-time investor, is a property with high maintenance. Amenities like pools also create additional expenses for supplies, services, and liability insurance. When you have a property with special features, it is hard to control expenses because so many unforeseen things can go wrong.

2. Low Rents

Investment property values are primarily based on income. As income increases, the market value of the property goes up. Therefore, a property with low rents has the potential to not only increase your income, but the base value of the property as well. It is called in the trade, a "value-added" opportunity. You make money by buying the property and increasing the rents.

> TIP: When buying a property with low rents, make sure the price is based on actual rents, not pro forma income.

3. Property Needs Repairs

The principle is similar to fixer-uppers in single family homes. You need to buy at a price where, after necessary repairs, you can still be below the market value of the property. Commercial property is different, though, because it is strictly an investment. If you know what you are doing, this is a good way to create additional value. Usually the seller either doesn't want to, or can't make these repairs, so you should get a better price.

4. Location

Remember the three rules for buying real estate—location, location, location? Well, they apply even more to investment property. It significantly affects value because properties in the best locations (called A locations) command higher rents, which create higher property values.

You can buy a property for less in a marginal or undesirable area, but you will be better off in the long run in a good area. It will be easier to finance and easier to sell when the time comes. Your property will also appreciate faster.

The one thing you want to consider is how far from your home you want the property to be. The rule of thumb for most investors is that the property should be no more than one hour away from their house. Nobody wants to drive for hours just to check on property.

TIP: Some sophisticated investors say the hour away can be by plane.

When you finish touring, reevaluate your list of properties and eliminate those that don't match your goals. When you have a list of acceptable properties, go to Step 5.

area, but you will be better off in the long-run in a good area. It will be easier to finance and easier to sell when the time comes. Your property will also appreciate faster.

The one thing you want to consider is how far from your home you want the property to be. The rule of thumb for most investors is that the property should be no more than one hour from their home. Nobody wants to drive for hours just to focus on property.

The More Sophisticated Investor, or Say the Investor who wants to make by plan

When you think too much to invest, when it is, they you start thinking about thought that you need to create a list of keep as a computer systems.

Select a Property

Now you need to review the properties that made the cut and evaluate them against your goals. This is where you crunch the numbers in earnest.

1. Verify that income shown is actual and not projected.
2. Compare the properties you selected on the following points:

Property 1   Property 2   Property 3

- Price
- Location:
  A- location = Excellent
  B- location = Good
  C- location = Average
- Appearance:
  Excellent
  Good
  Average
- Overall condition:
  Excellent
  Good
  Average

- Deferred maintenance
  Yes/No, Cost
- Rent roll
- Income
- Expenses
- Net Income
- Cap Rate

There is usually one property that stands out from the rest. If not, use your best judgment as to which property is best for you. After you have selected the right property, you can move on to Step 6

Close the Deal

F IRST THING IS TO WRITE an offer on the property you chose. Your broker will make the offer for you, but you have to determine the price and terms to submit. Commercial offers are usually submitted with a Letter of Intent (LOI).

Don't make a Low-ball offer. That will offend the seller. I have seen many instances where the seller refuses to even respond to a low offer. If you use this tactic, you could be lumped in a category of buyers called "bottom feeders, a pretty negative term. Even if the seller does respond to your offer, he will have his back up, and it will be difficult to negotiate. You would be far better off making a reasonable offer.

If your offer is full price, then the only negotiating will be on terms. If you are not involved with competing offers, you may have to make one or more counter-offers to agree with the seller on price and terms.

If you become involved in a multiple-offer situation, I have a surefire way to win the battle. Send me an email and I will divulge it to you. My address is listed in the Summary.

Once you have a signed contract, you can start the due-diligence process.

1. **Submit your loan application** with the property address. You should already have a pre-approval letter from your lender which was submitted to the seller with your offer. The lender now will go through the approval process with the property.
2. **Conduct a physical inspection** – Hire a reliable, qualified inspector to do the physical inspection, and be present while it is being done. That way you have a firsthand look at the items the inspector will note. Depending on what he finds, he may recommend further inspections, like a roof inspection, a geological inspection, a structural inspection, or an environmental inspection.
3. **Request repairs** – Review the physical inspection report with your broker and decide what repairs you want made. Your broker will submit a repair request based on the items you want to be repaired, and deliver it to the seller.
4. **Review all due-diligence documentation**- the following items should have been requested from the seller with your offer. Have your team review and evaluate them for you:

   • Lease agreements
   • Income and expense statements
   • Environmental studies
   • Maintenance and service contracts
   • Architectural and engineering plans
   • Number of parking spaces
   • Property lines and boundaries
   • Property zoning and uses

5. **Conduct a final walk-through** – Before closing, check to see if the requested repairs have been made, and that the property is in the same condition as it was when you made your offer.

6. **Sign your loan documents-** Send the balance of your down payment to closing. Your loan will generally fund in 48 hours and the sale will record the next day.

Congratulations!

You are now a real estate investor on your way to living your Big Dream.

STEP 7

Create Your Success Plan

So YOU OWN AN INVESTMENT property-what should you do next?

The first thing you should do is hire a competent property manager. This is not something you want to do yourself. There are many facets involved:

- Knowing how to repair anything from a toilet to an air-conditioner
- Collecting rents
- Evicting tenants
- Legal issues dealing with tenants
- Screening tenants
- Knowing whom to call in emergencies
- Paying all the expenses on time
- Maintaining properties to comply with city codes
- Dealing with government agencies

Learning on the job is not the best way to go. Hire a competent property management company,

Management Nightmare

One of our investment agents, Allen, sold an eight-unit apartment building to his clients, Barry and Karen. After the transaction closed, he asked if they would like recommendations for a property management company.

Barry replied that it wasn't all that difficult; he was going to do it himself.

Allen cautioned him about the pitfalls of personally managing the property, but Barry was insistent. Wishing them good luck, Allen told them to call him if he could be of help.

About seven months later, Allen received a call from Barry. He sounded rattled and out of breath. Allen asked what was wrong, and Barry talked non-stop for 20 minutes.

Barry told him that the very first week, they received a call from a tenant at midnight on Sunday. His toilet was overflowing and flooding his apartment.

A sleepy Barry got dressed and rushed over to fix the problem. It turns out that he couldn't, so he turned off the water to the toilet and told the tenant he would have a plumber repair it the next day. Now he had to find a plumber.

By the middle of the next month, two of the tenants had not paid their rent. Barry went over to see them. One said he had mailed the check, and the other said he was just laid off from his job and could no longer afford the rent.

Of course, the "check in the mail" never came. Now Barry was in the position of having to evict two of his eight tenants, without a clue about how to do it. In the meantime, he was receiving no income from them. He *was* smart enough, however, to hire an eviction attorney to handle it.

The tenant in unit # 2 knew the ropes. After receiving his Three-Day Notice to Quit or Pay Rent, he filed for bankruptcy. It took five months to get him out of the apartment and required the services of a U.S. Marshall.

The other tenant moved out in 60 days. When Barry inspected the unit after the tenant had left, he was stunned. The window coverings were gone, the carpeting was ruined, and the built-in appliances were destroyed, along with countless other items. In the end it cost over $4,000 to restore the unit to rentable condition.

To accomplish this, Barry had to hire all the required contractors and supervise their work.

He then put an ad in the paper and started interviewing prospective tenants. When he began verifying their information, he found that some were lying. Finding good tenants was harder than he'd thought.

The final straw was when he received a call from the Fair Housing Agency of the federal government. Someone had filed a complaint because he didn't rent them an apartment. He had to go to a hearing to defend himself. That's when he called Allen.

Allen asked how he could help, and Barry said he needed a good property management company. He was more than ready to hire one. Not only had he spent too much time away from his job, the stress had become unbearable.

Allen gave him two companies to call, and Barry hired one of them.

Three months later, Allen received a call from Barry. He sounded calm and invited Allen to dinner to show his appreciation for his recommendations.

Barry said it was a huge relief to get the burden of management off his back, and he was now devoting more time to his job. He also said hiring a property manager was one of the best decisions he'd ever made.

Here's the Magic

Owning commercial income producing property creates wealth over time and is definitely worth pursuing.

Here are some of the key elements for success:

- Adopt a long term approach; this is a marathon, not a sprint
- Develop an investment mentality, not an "instant gratification life" like so many Americans (drive an older car but own a duplex)
- Put the cash flow back into the property to either reduce the debt or to improve financial productivity

The resulting wealth building benefits are really magical:

- Someone else is paying your debt (the tenants rent makes the payment on the property)
- If the loan is amortizing, the principal reduction is yours (debt relief)
- You get to keep what is left over each month (cash flow)
- You get the appreciation in value over time
- You get the depreciation on your tax return to reduce your taxes
- Many of your expenses can be written off against your income if they are related to the property and its operation

More Magic

Here is another approach which is being used by many of my clients, use the positive cash flow of your investment to pay off your loan sooner.

Using the industrial property example in figure 7.1, the annual cash flow is $30,000. Added to your annual principal reduction of $10,000, you can reduce your loan amount by $40,000 per year. This would pay off your loan in about 16 years.

If you purchased a second property in year five, you could start paying down that mortgage by $30,000 a year plus the principal reduction of $10,000. When the first property is paid off in 11 more years, you can then use the total income of $72,000 from that property to pay down the second property loan. Together with the $30,000 plus the $10,000 in principal reduction on the second property, it would be paid off in 15 years.

(Note: This does not include any rental increases, which would probably occur, that would further accelerate the payoff.)

(If you don't have enough down payment to buy the second property, you can refinance the first property to get the funds. This will just extend the process, but you will still become rich.)

The bottom line is that in 20 years you would own two Investment properties free and clear. You cash flow would be $72,000 X 2 = $144,000 per year. And, your two properties would be worth about $4,000,000 based on the 6.34% average annual appreciation rate. This is assuming that no property depreciation occurs during that period.

(Note: Again, this does not include any rental increases, which could amount to 2-4% per year, that would increase your cash flow by that amount.)

Recent surveys show you need $2.4 million net worth to be considered wealthy.

Under this scenario you would be considered rich.

Then, if you wanted to, you can buy a third property and pay it off in seven years, using the cash flow of the other two properties.

However, if you wanted to get started on your Big Dream today, you could use the $30,000 annual flow from your first investment to get started. This number would increase by about an average of 2% per year, based on current projections by NAR, until the 16th year, when it will go to $72,000 plus the rental increases because the loan will be paid off.

In the end, passive income can make "work optional" for you and that is the greatest magic of all.

*Please note: This is just an example of what could be done. It is in no way a prediction of what you could do. These numbers represent what is possible. It is up to you to determine how far you could go.

Summary

"Your greatest self has been waiting your whole life.
Don't make it wait any longer."
-- Steve Maraboli

IT IS NOT HARD TO get started in investment real estate, but you need to follow the "New Rules."

Rule #1. Work with an experienced investment broker.
Rule #2. Don't buy a property based on projected revenue, buy only on actual income.
Rule #3. Cash flow is king.
Rule #4. Buy based only on the numbers, not on emotion.

Here is a summary of the steps you need to take to create income and wealth:

Step 1: Learn the Basics
Step 2: Assemble Your Team
Step 3: Develop a Plan
Step 4: Preview and Evaluate Properties
Step 5: Select Property
Step 6: Close the Deal
Step 7: Create Your Success Plan

If you followed this plan, you are now free do whatever you want. What is your Big Dream? If you are not sure, send me an email (address below) and I will send you a mini-course called,*" How to Live Your Dream Life*," absolutely free.

But if you do know, you should be really excited because you now have the resources to make it happen. Don't wait any longer. Start today.

I am rooting for you.

Best wishes for your success,
H.Richard Steinhoff
http:www.hrichardsteinhoff.com
hrichardsteinhoff@att.net

P.S. If you liked my book, please go to www.amazon.com/books and leave a review.

ABOUT THE AUTHOR

H. Richard Steinhoff is an author, speaker, and community leader dedicated to improving people's lives. During his 35 years as a real estate broker, he has helped hundreds of clients achieve their real estate goals.

His real estate background includes serving as president of the Orange County Broker Council, president of the Broker Council of Southern California, vice-president and director of the Board of Realtors, director of the California Association of Realtors, as well as membership in the National Association of Realtors. He was made an *Honorary Member for Life* by the California Association of Realtors.

. His community involvement has included serving as vice-president and director of the Chamber of Commerce; president of Center 500 (a major fundraising organization for the Segerstrom Center for the Arts in Orange County); ex-officio director of the Segerstrom Center, for the Arts; director of the Laguna Niguel Community Council; president of The Club at Rancho Niguel; president of the Crown Royale Homeowner's Association; chairman of the Investment Advisory Commission, City of Mission Viejo; as well as being a member of the Chancellor's Club of the University of California, the Irvine Exchange Club, and the California State University Alumni Association.

Richard has been a featured guest on talk radio shows in cities that include Cleveland; New Orleans; Chicago; Baltimore;

Charlotte; Phoenix; and many in California, New York, and Florida; along with several television news programs, including Fox Evening News in Los Angeles. He was also a featured speaker at the National Association of Realtors Annual Convention.

He has received the *Man of the Year Award* from the Irvine Chamber of Commerce, the *President's Award* from the Muscular Dystrophy Association, and has been listed in "Who's Who in California" as well as "Who's Who in the West." He has also recently received a *Certificate of Recognition for Community Leadership* from the California State Legislature.

His education includes a Bachelor of Science degree in Business Administration from California State University and a Certificate in Industrial Relations from the UCLA Graduate School of Business. Richard is also a member of the American Mensa Society

FREE BONUS GIFT

As a thank you for purchasing this book, H. Richard Steinhoff is offering you the following FREE gift:

My Bucket List Kit

It has everything you need to finally complete your list of things you want to do before you die.

The kit includes:

1. Forms
2. Instructions
3. An example of a completed list with suggestions

To claim your free gift, go to: http://gooo.gl/VqxEaf

RESOURCES BY
H. RICHARD STEINHOFF

Real Estate Investing 101: Best Way to Buy a House and Save Big, Top 20 Tips (Volume 1)

Real Estate Investing 101: Best Way to Sell a House Fast for Top Dollar, Top 14 Tips (Volume 2)

Real Estate Investing 101: Best Way to Save Money on a Good Home Loan, Top 13 tips (Volume 3)

Real Estate Investing 101: Best New Short Sale Solutions, Top 10 Tips (Volume 4)

Real Estate Investing 101: Best New Foreclosure Solutions, Top 10 Tips (Volume 5)

Real Estate Investing 101: Best Way to Invest for Big Returns,Top 10 Tips (Volume 6)

Real Estate Investing 101: Best Way to Find a Good Real Estate Agent, Top 13 Tips. (Volume 7)

Turning Myths into Money: An Insider's Guide to Winning the Real Estate Game

Dying On Purpose: How My Near Death Experience Can Change Your Life

Live Your Dream Life: A Step-By-Step Plan

GLOSSARY

A

"A" Loan or "A" Paper: a credit rating where the FICO score is 660 or above. There have been no late mortgage payments within a 12-month period. This is the best credit rating to have when entering into a new loan.

ARM: Adjustable Rate Mortgage; a mortgage loan subject to changes in interest rates; when rates change, ARM monthly payments increase or decrease at intervals determined by the lender; the change in monthly payment amount, however, is usually subject to a cap.

Abstract of Title: documents recording the ownership of property throughout time.

Acceleration: the right of the lender to demand payment on the outstanding balance of a loan.

Acceptance: the written approval of the buyer's offer by the seller.

Additional Principal Payment: money paid to the lender in addition to the established payment amount used directly against the loan principal to shorten the length of the loan.

Adjustable-Rate Mortgage (ARM): a mortgage loan that does not have a fixed interest rate. During the life of the loan the interest rate will change based on the index rate. Also referred to as adjustable mortgage loans (AMLs) or variable-rate mortgages (VRMs).

Adjustment Date: the actual date that the interest rate is changed for an ARM.

Adjustment Index: the published market index used to calculate the interest rate of an ARM at the time of origination or adjustment.

Adjustment Interval: the time between the interest rate change and the monthly payment for an ARM. The interval is usually every one, three or five years depending on the index.

Affidavit: a signed, sworn statement made by the buyer or seller regarding the truth of information provided.

Amenity: a feature of the home or property that serves as a benefit to the buyer but that is not necessary to its use; may be natural (like location, woods, water) or man-made (like a swimming pool or garden).

American Society of Home Inspectors: the American Society of Home Inspectors is a professional association of independent home inspectors. Phone: (800) 743-2744

Amortization: a payment plan that enables you to reduce your debt gradually through monthly payments. The payments may be principal and interest, or interest-only. The monthly amount is based on the schedule for the entire term or length of the loan.

Annual Mortgagor Statement: yearly statement to borrowers detailing the remaining principal and amounts paid for taxes and interest.

Annual Percentage Rate (APR): a measure of the cost of credit, expressed as a yearly rate. It includes interest as well as other charges. Because all lenders, by federal law, follow the same rules to ensure the accuracy of the annual percentage rate, it provides consumers with a good basis for comparing the cost of loans, including mortgage plans. APR is a higher rate than the simple interest of the mortgage.

Application: the first step in the official loan approval process; this form is used to record important information about the potential borrower necessary to the underwriting process.

Application Fee: a fee charged by lenders to process a loan application.

Appraisal: a document from a professional that gives an estimate of a property's fair market value based on the sales of comparable homes in the area and the features of a property; an appraisal is generally required by a lender before loan approval to ensure that the mortgage loan amount is not more than the value of the property.

Appraisal Fee: fee charged by an appraiser to estimate the market value of a property.

Appraised Value: an estimation of the current market value of a property.

Appraiser: a qualified individual who uses his or her experience and knowledge to prepare the appraisal estimate.

Appreciation: an increase in property value.

Arbitration: a legal method of resolving a dispute without going to court.

As-is Condition: the purchase or sale of a property in its existing condition without repairs.

Asking Price: a seller's stated price for a property.

Assessed Value: the value that a public official has placed on any asset (used to determine taxes).

Assessments: the method of placing value on an asset for taxation purposes.

Assessor: a government official who is responsible for determining the value of a property for the purpose of taxation.

Assets: any item with measurable value.

Assumable Mortgage: when a home is sold, the seller may be able to transfer the mortgage to the new buyer. This means the mortgage is assumable. Lenders generally require a credit review of the new borrower and may charge a fee for the assumption. Some mortgages contain a due-on-sale clause, which means that the mortgage may not be transferable to a new buyer. Instead, the lender may make you pay the entire balance that is due when you sell the home. An assumable mortgage can help you attract buyers if you sell your home.

Assumption Clause: a provision in the terms of a loan that allows the buyer to take legal responsibility for the mortgage from the seller.

Automated Underwriting: loan processing completed through a computer-based system that evaluates past credit history to determine if a loan should be approved. This system removes the possibility of personal bias against the buyer.

B

"B" Loan or "B" Paper: FICO scores from 620 - 659. Factors include two 30 day late mortgage payments and two to three 30 day late installment loan payments in the last 12 months. No delinquencies over 60 days are allowed. Should be two to four years since a bankruptcy. Also referred to as Sub-Prime.

Back End Ratio (debt ratio): a ratio that compares the total of all monthly debt payments (mortgage, real estate taxes and insurance, car loans, and other consumer loans) to gross monthly income.

Back to Back Escrow: arrangements that an owner makes to oversee the sale of one property and the purchase of another at the same time.

Back-up Offer: an offer that is accepted by the Seller and placed in second position behind the first accepted offer.

Balance Sheet: a financial statement that shows the assets, liabilities and net worth of an individual or company.

Balloon Loan or Mortgage: a mortgage that typically offers low rates for an initial period of time (usually 5, 7, or 10) years; after that time period elapses, the balance is due or is refinanced by the borrower.

Balloon Payment: the final lump sum payment due at the end of a balloon mortgage.

Bankruptcy: a federal law whereby a person's assets are turned over to a trustee and used to pay off outstanding debts; this usually occurs when someone owes more than they have the ability to repay.

Biweekly Payment Mortgage: a mortgage paid twice a month instead of once a month, reducing the amount of interest to be paid on the loan.

Borrower: a person who has been approved to receive a loan and is then obligated to repay it and any additional fees according to the loan terms.

Bridge Loan: a short-term loan paid back relatively fast. Normally used until a long-term loan can be processed.

Broker: a licensed individual or firm that charges a fee to serve as the mediator between the buyer and seller. Mortgage brokers are individuals in the business of arranging funding or negotiating contracts for a client, but who does not loan the money. A real estate broker is someone who helps find a house.

Broker's Price Opinion (BPO): a Broker's written opinion of the current market value of a property. This is usually done for lenders prior to foreclosure on a property.

Building Code: based on agreed upon safety standards within a specific area, a building code is a regulation that determines the design, construction, and materials used in building.

Budget: a detailed record of all income earned and spent during a specific period of time.

Live Your Big Dream

Buy Down: the seller pays an amount to the lender so the lender provides a lower rate and lower payments many times for an ARM. The seller may increase the sales price to cover the cost of the buy down.

C

"C" Loan or "C" Paper: FICO scores typically from 580 to 619. Factors include three to four 30 day late mortgage payments and four to six 30 day late installment loan payments or two to four 60 day late payments. Should be one to two years since bankruptcy. Also referred to as Sub - Prime.

Callable Debt: a debt security whose issuer has the right to redeem the security at a specified price on or after a specified date, but prior to its stated final maturity.

Cap: a limit, such as one placed on an adjustable rate mortgage, on how much a monthly payment or interest rate can increase or decrease, either at each adjustment period or during the life of the mortgage. Payment caps do not limit the amount of interest the lender is earning, so they may cause negative amortization.

Capacity: The ability to make mortgage payments on time, dependant on assets and the amount of income each month after paying housing costs, debts and other obligations.

Capital Gain: the profit received based on the difference of the original purchase price and the total sale price.

Capital Improvements: property improvements that either will enhance the property value or will increase the useful life of the property.

Capital or Cash Reserves: an individual's savings, investments, or assets.

Cash-Out Refinance: when a borrower refinances a mortgage at a higher principal amount to get additional money. Usually this occurs when the property has appreciated in value. For example, if a home has a current value of $100,000 and an outstanding mortgage of $60,000, the owner could refinance $80,000 and have additional $20,000 in cash.

Cash Reserves: a cash amount sometimes required of the buyer to be held in reserve in addition to the down payment and closing costs; the amount is determined by the lender.

Casualty Protection: property insurance that covers any damage to the home and personal property either inside or outside the home.

Certificate of Title: a document provided by a qualified source, such as a title company, that shows the property legally belongs to the current owner; before the title is transferred at closing, it should be clear and free of all liens or other claims.

Chapter 7 Bankruptcy: a bankruptcy that requires assets be liquidated in exchange for the cancellation of debt.

Chapter 13 Bankruptcy: this type of bankruptcy sets a payment plan between the borrower and the creditor monitored by the court. The homeowner can keep the property, but must make payments according to the court's terms within a 3 to 5 year period.

Charge-Off: the portion of principal and interest due on a loan that is written off when deemed to be uncollectible.

Clear Title: a property title that has no defects. Properties with clear titles are marketable for sale.

Closing: the final step in property purchase where the title is transferred from the seller to the buyer. Closing occurs at a meeting between the buyer, seller, settlement agent, and other agents. At the closing the seller receives payment for the property. Also known as settlement.

Closing Costs: fees for final property transfer not included in the price of the property. Typical closing costs include charges for the mortgage loan such as origination fees, discount points, appraisal fee, survey, title insurance, legal fees, real estate professional fees, prepayment of taxes and insurance, and real estate transfer taxes. A common estimate of a Buyer's closing costs is 2 to 4 percent of the purchase price of the home. A common estimate for Seller's closing costs is 3 to 9 percent.

Cloud On The Title: any condition which affects the clear title to real property.

Co-Borrower: an additional person that is responsible for loan repayment and is listed on the title.

Co-Signed Account: an account signed by someone in addition to the primary borrower, making both people responsible for the amount borrowed.

Co-Signer: a person that signs a credit application with another person, agreeing to be equally responsible for the repayment of the loan.

Collateral: security in the form of money or property pledged for the payment of a loan. For example, on a home loan, the

H. Richard Steinhoff

home is the collateral and can be taken away from the borrower if mortgage payments are not made.

Collection Account: an unpaid debt referred to a collection agency to collect on the bad debt. This type of account is reported to the credit bureau and will show on the borrower's credit report.

Commission: an amount, usually a percentage of the property sales price that is collected by a real estate professional as a fee for negotiating the transaction. Traditionally the home seller pays the commission.

Common Stock: a security that provides voting rights in a corporation and pays a dividend after preferred stock holders have been paid. This is the most common stock held within a company.

Comparative Market Analysis (CMA): a property evaluation that determines property value by comparing similar properties sold within the last year.

Compensating Factors: factors that show the ability to repay a loan based on less traditional criteria, such as employment, rent, and utility payment history.

Condominium: a form of ownership in which individuals purchase and own a unit of housing in a multi-unit complex. The owner also shares financial responsibility for common areas.

Conforming loan: is a loan that does not exceed Fannie Mae's and Freddie Mac's loan limits. Freddie Mac and Fannie Mae loans are referred to as conforming loans.

74

Consideration: an item of value given in exchange for a promise or act.

Construction Loan: a short-term, to finance the cost of building a new home. The lender pays the builder based on milestones accomplished during the building process. For example, once a sub-contractor pours the foundation and it is approved by inspectors the lender will pay for their service.

Contingency: a clause in a purchase contract outlining conditions that must be fulfilled before the contract is executed. Both, buyer or seller may include contingencies in a contract, but both parties must accept the contingency.

Conventional Loan: a private sector loan, one that is not guaranteed or insured by the U.S. government.

Conversion Clause: a provision in some ARMs allowing it to change to a fixed-rate loan at some point during the term. Usually conversions are allowed at the end of the first adjustment period. At the time of the conversion, the new fixed rate is generally set at one of the rates then prevailing for fixed rate mortgages. There may be additional cost for this clause.

Convertible ARM: an adjustable-rate mortgage that provides the borrower the ability to convert to a fixed-rate within a specified time.

Cooperative (Co-op): residents purchase stock in a cooperative corporation that owns a structure; each stockholder is then entitled to live in a specific unit of the structure and is responsible for paying a portion of the loan.

Cost of Funds Index (COFI): an index used to determine interest rate changes for some adjustable-rate mortgages.

Counter Offer: a rejection to all or part of a purchase offer that negotiates different terms to reach an acceptable sales contract.

Covenants: legally enforceable terms that govern the use of property. These terms are transferred with the property deed. Discriminatory covenants are illegal and unenforceable. Also known as a condition, restriction, deed restriction or restrictive covenant.

Credit: an agreement that a person will borrow money and repay it to the lender over time.

Credit Bureau: an agency that provides financial information and payment history to lenders about potential borrowers. Also known as a National Credit Repository.

Credit Counseling: education on how to improve bad credit and how to avoid having more debt than can be repaid.

Credit Enhancement: a method used by a lender to reduce default of a loan by requiring collateral, mortgage insurance, or other agreements.

Credit Grantor: the lender that provides a loan or credit.

Credit History: a record of an individual that lists all debts and the payment history for each. The report that is generated from the history is called a credit report. Lenders use this information to gauge a potential borrower's ability to repay a loan.

Credit Loss Ratio: the ratio of credit-related losses to the dollar amount of MBS outstanding and total mortgages owned by the corporation.

Credit Related Expenses: foreclosed property expenses plus the provision for losses.

Credit Related Losses: foreclosed property expenses combined with charge-offs.

Credit Repair Companies: Private, for-profit businesses that claim to offer consumers credit and debt repayment difficulties assistance with their credit problems and a bad credit report.

Credit Report: a report generated by the credit bureau that contains the borrower's credit history for the past seven years. Lenders use this information to determine if a loan will be granted.

Credit Risk: a term used to describe the possibility of default on a loan by a borrower.

Credit Score: a score calculated by using a person's credit report to determine the likelihood of a loan being repaid on time. Scores range from about 360 - 840: a lower score meaning a person is a higher risk, while a higher score means that there is less risk.

Credit Union: a non-profit financial institution federally regulated and owned by the members or people who use their services. Credit unions serve groups that hold a common interest and you have to become a member to use the available services.

Creditor: the lending institution providing a loan or credit.

Creditworthiness: the way a lender measures the ability of a person to qualify and repay a loan.

D

Debtor: The person or entity that borrows money. The term debtor may be used interchangeably with the term borrower.

Debt-to-Income Ratio: a comparison or ratio of gross income to housing and non-housing expenses; With the FHA, the monthly mortgage payment should be no more than 29% of monthly gross income (before taxes) and the mortgage payment combined with non-housing debts should not exceed 41% of income.

Debt Security: a security that represents a loan from an investor to an issuer. The issuer in turn agrees to pay interest in addition to the principal amount borrowed.

Deductible: the amount of cash payment that is made by the insured (the homeowner) to cover a portion of a damage or loss. Sometimes also called "out-of-pocket expenses." For example, out of a total damage claim of $1,000, the homeowner might pay a $250 deductible toward the loss, while the insurance company pays $750 toward the loss. Typically, the higher the deductible, the lower the cost of the policy.

Deed: a document that legally transfers ownership of property from one person to another. The deed is recorded on public record with the property description and the owner's signature. Also known as the title.

Deed-in-Lieu: to avoid foreclosure ("in lieu" of foreclosure), a deed is given to the lender to fulfill the obligation to repay the debt; this process does not allow the borrower to remain in the house but helps avoid the costs, time, and effort associated with foreclosure.

Default: the inability to make timely monthly mortgage payments or otherwise comply with mortgage terms. A loan is considered in default when payment has not been paid after 60 to 90 days. Once in default the lender can exercise legal rights defined in the contract to begin foreclosure proceedings

Delinquency: failure of a borrower to make timely mortgage payments under a loan agreement. Generally after fifteen days a late fee may be assessed.

Deposit (Earnest Money): money put down by a potential buyer to show that they are serious about purchasing the home; it becomes part of the down payment if the offer is accepted, is returned if the offer is rejected, or is forfeited if the buyer pulls out of the deal. During the contingency period the money may be returned to the buyer if the contingencies are not met to the buyer's satisfaction.

Depreciation: a decrease in the value or price of a property due to changes in market conditions, wear and tear on the property, or other factors.

Derivative: a contract between two or more parties where the security is dependent on the price of another investment.

Disclosures: the release of relevant information about a property that may influence the final sale, especially if it represents defects or problems. "Full disclosure" usually refers to the responsibility of the seller to voluntarily provide all known information about the property. Some disclosures may be required by law, such as the federal requirement to warn of potential lead-based paint hazards in pre-1978 housing. A seller found to have knowingly lied about a defect may face legal penalties.

Discount Point: normally paid at closing and generally calculated to be equivalent to 1% of the total loan amount, discount points are paid to reduce the interest rate on a loan. In an ARM with an initial rate discount, the lender gives up a number of percentage points in interest to give you a lower rate and lower payments for part of the mortgage term (usually for one year or less). After the discount period, the ARM rate will probably go up depending on the index rate.

Down Payment: the portion of a home's purchase price that is paid in cash and is not part of the mortgage loan. This amount varies based on the loan type, but is determined by taking the difference of the sale price and the actual mortgage loan amount. Mortgage insurance is required when a down payment less than 20 percent is made.

Document Recording: after closing on a loan, certain documents are filed and made public record. Discharges for the prior mortgage holder are filed first. Then the deed is filed with the new owner's and mortgage company's names.

Due on Sale Clause: a provision of a loan allowing the lender to demand full repayment of the loan if the property is sold.

Duration: the number of years it will take to receive the present value of all future payments on a security to include both principal and interest.

E

Earnest Money (Deposit): money put down by a potential buyer to show that they are serious about purchasing the home; it becomes part of the down payment if the offer is accepted, is returned if the offer is rejected, or is forfeited if the buyer pulls out of the deal. During the contingency period the money may be returned to the buyer if the contingencies are not met to the buyer's satisfaction.

Earnings Per Share (EPS): a corporation's profit that is divided among each share of common stock. It is determined by taking the net earnings divided by the number of outstanding common stocks held. This is a way that a company reports profitability.

Easements: the legal rights that give someone other than the owner access to use property for a specific purpose. Easements may affect property values and are sometimes a part of the deed.

EEM: Energy Efficient Mortgage; an FHA program that helps homebuyers save money on utility bills by enabling them to finance the cost of adding energy efficiency features to a new or existing home as part of the home purchase

Eminent Domain: when a government takes private property for public use. The owner receives payment for its fair market value. The property can then proceed to condemnation proceedings.

Encroachments: a structure that extends over the legal property line on to another individual's property. The property surveyor will note any encroachment on the lot survey done before property transfer. The person who owns the structure will be asked to remove it to prevent future problems.

Encumbrance: anything that affects title to a property, such as loans, leases, easements, or restrictions.

Equal Credit Opportunity Act (ECOA): a federal law requiring lenders to make credit available equally without discrimination based on race, color, religion, national origin, age, sex, marital status, or receipt of income from public assistance programs.

Equity: an owner's financial interest in a property; calculated by subtracting the amount still owed on the mortgage loon(s)from the fair market value of the property.

Escape Clause: a provision in a purchase contract that allows either party to cancel part or the entire contract if the other does not respond to changes to the sale within a set period. The most common use of the escape clause is if the buyer makes the purchase offer contingent on the sale of another house.

Escrow: funds held in an account to be used by the lender to pay for home insurance and property taxes. The funds may also be held by a third party until contractual conditions are met and then paid out.

Escrow Account/Impound Account: a separate account into which the lender puts a portion of each monthly mortgage payment; an escrow account provides the funds needed for such expenses as property taxes, homeowners insurance, mortgage insurance, etc.

Estate: the ownership interest of a person in real property. The sum total of all property, real and personal, owned by a person.

Exclusive Listing: a written contract giving a real estate agent the exclusive right to sell a property for a specific timeframe.

F

FICO Score: FICO is an abbreviation for Fair Isaac Corporation and refers to a person's credit score based on credit history.

Lenders and credit card companies use the number to decide if the person is likely to pay his or her bills. A credit score is evaluated using information from the three major credit bureaus and is usually between 300 and 850.

FSBO (For Sale by Owner): a home that is offered for sale by the owner without the benefit of a real estate professional.

Fair Credit Reporting Act: federal act to ensure that credit bureaus are fair and accurate protecting the individual's privacy rights enacted in 1971 and revised in October 1997.

Fair Housing Act: a law that prohibits discrimination in all facets of the home buying process on the basis of race, color, national origin, religion, sex, familial status, or disability.

Fair Market Value: : the hypothetical price that a willing buyer and seller will agree upon when they are acting freely, carefully, and with complete knowledge of the situation.

Familial Status: HUD uses this term to describe a single person, a pregnant woman or a household with children under 18 living with parents or legal custodians who might experience housing discrimination.

Fannie Mae: Federal National Mortgage Association (FNMA); a federally-chartered enterprise owned by private stockholders that purchases residential mortgages and converts them into securities for sale to investors; by purchasing mortgages, Fannie Mae supplies funds that lenders may loan to potential homebuyers. Also known as a Government Sponsored Enterprise (GSE).

FHA: Federal Housing Administration; established in 1934 to advance homeownership opportunities for all Americans;

assists homebuyers by providing mortgage insurance to lenders to cover most losses that may occur when a borrower defaults; this encourages lenders to make loans to borrowers who might not qualify for conventional mortgages.

First Mortgage: the mortgage with first priority if the loan is not paid.

Fixed Expenses: payments that do not vary from month to month.

Fixed-Rate Mortgage: a mortgage with payments that remain the same throughout the life of the loan because the interest rate and other terms are fixed and do not change.

Fixture: personal property permanently attached to real estate or real property that becomes a part of the real estate.

Float: the act of allowing an interest rate and discount points to fluctuate with changes in the market.

Flood Insurance: insurance that protects homeowners against losses from a flood; if a home is located in a flood plain, the lender will require flood insurance before approving a loan.

Forbearance: a lender may decide not to take legal action when a borrower is late in making a payment. Usually this occurs when a borrower sets up a plan that both sides agree will bring overdue mortgage payments up to date.

Foreclosure: a legal process in which mortgaged property is sold to pay the loan of the defaulting borrower. Foreclosure laws are based on the statutes of each state.

Freddie Mac: Federal Home Loan Mortgage Corporation (FHLM); a federally chartered corporation that purchases residential mortgages, securitizes them, and sells them to investors; this provides lenders with funds for new homebuyers. Also known as a Government Sponsored Enterprise (GSE).

Front End Ratio: a percentage comparing a borrower's total monthly cost to buy a house (mortgage principal and interest, insurance, and real estate taxes) to monthly income before deductions.

G

GSE: abbreviation for government sponsored enterprises: a collection of financial services corporations formed by the United States Congress to reduce interest rates for farmers and homeowners. Examples include Fannie Mae and Freddie Mac.

Ginnie Mae: Government National Mortgage Association (GNMA); a government-owned corporation overseen by the U.S. Department of Housing and Urban Development, Ginnie Mae pools FHA-insured and VA-guaranteed loans to back securities for private investment; as With Fannie Mae and Freddie Mac, the investment income provides funding that may then be lent to eligible borrowers by lenders.

Global Debt Facility: designed to allow investors all over the world to purchase debt (loans) of U.S. dollar and foreign currency through a variety of clearing systems.

Good Faith Estimate: an estimate of all closing fees including pre-paid and escrow items as well as lender charges; must be given to the borrower within three days after submission of a loan application.

Graduated Payment Mortgages: mortgages that begin with lower monthly payments that get slowly larger over a period of years, eventually reaching a fixed level and remaining there for the life of the loan. Graduated payment loans may be good if you expect your annual income to increase.

Grantee: an individual to whom an interest in real property is conveyed.

Grantor: an individual conveying an interest in real property.

Gross Income: money earned before taxes and other deductions. Sometimes it may include income from self-employment, rental property, alimony, child support, public assistance payments, and retirement benefits.

Guaranty Fee: payment to FannieMae from a lender for the assurance of timely principal and interest payments to MBS (Mortgage Backed Security) security holders.

H

HECM (Reverse Mortgage): the reverse mortgage is used by senior homeowners age 62 and older to convert the equity in their home into monthly streams of income and/or a line of credit to be repaid when they no longer occupy the home. A lending institution such as a mortgage lender, bank, credit union or savings and loan association funds the FHA insured loan, commonly known as HECM.

Hazard Insurance: protection against a specific loss, such as fire, wind etc., over a period of time that is secured by the payment of a regularly scheduled premium.

HELP: Homebuyer Education Learning Program; an educational program from the FHA that counsels people about the home buying process; HELP covers topics like budgeting, finding a home, getting a loan, and home maintenance; in most cases, completion of the program may entitle the homebuyer to a reduced initial FHA mortgage insurance premium-from 2.25% to 1.75% of the home purchase price.

Home Equity Line of Credit: a mortgage loan, usually in second mortgage, allowing a borrower to obtain cash against the equity of a home, up to a predetermined amount.

Home Equity Loan: a loan backed by the value of a home (real estate). If the borrower defaults or does not pay the loan, the lender has some rights to the property. The borrower can usually claim a home equity loan as a tax deduction.

Home Inspection: an examination of the structure and mechanical systems to determine a home's quality, soundness and safety; makes the potential homebuyer aware of any repairs that may be needed. The homebuyer generally pays inspection fees.

Home Warranty: offers protection for mechanical systems and attached appliances against unexpected repairs not covered by homeowner's insurance; coverage extends over a specific time period and does not cover the home's structure.

Homeowner's Insurance: an insurance policy, also called hazard insurance, that combines protection against damage to a dwelling and its contents including fire, storms or other damages with protection against claims of negligence or inappropriate action that result in someone's injury or property damage. Most lenders require homeowners insurance and may escrow the cost.

Flood insurance is generally not included in standard policies and must be purchased separately.

Homeownership Education Classes: classes that stress the need to develop a strong credit history and offer information about how to get a mortgage approved, qualify for a loan, choose an affordable home, go through financing and closing processes, and avoid mortgage problems that cause people to lose their homes.

Homestead Credit: property tax credit program, offered by some state governments, that provides reductions in property taxes to eligible households.

Housing Counseling Agency: provides counseling and assistance to individuals on a variety of issues, including loan default, fair housing, and home buying.

HUD: the U.S. Department of Housing and Urban Development; established in 1965, HUD works to create a decent home and suitable living environment for all Americans; it does this by addressing housing needs, improving and developing American communities, and enforcing fair housing laws.

HUD1 Statement: also known as the "settlement sheet," or "closing statement" it itemizes all closing costs; must be given to the borrower at or before closing. Items that appear on the statement include real estate commissions, loan fees, points, and escrow amounts.

HVAC: Heating, Ventilation and Air Conditioning; a home's heating and cooling system.

I

Indemnification: to secure against any loss or damage, compensate or give security for reimbursement for loss or damage incurred. A homeowner should negotiate for inclusion of an indemnification provision in a contract with a general contractor or for a separate indemnity agreement protecting the homeowner from harm, loss or damage caused by actions or omissions of the general (and all sub) contractor.

Index: the measure of interest rate changes that the lender uses to decide how much the interest rate of an ARM will change over time. No one can be sure when an index rate will go up or down. If a lender bases interest rate adjustments on the average value of an index over time, your interest rate would not be as volatile. You should ask your lender how the index for any ARM you are considering has changed in recent years, and where it is reported.

Inflation: the number of dollars in circulation exceeds the amount of goods and services available for purchase; inflation results in a decrease in the dollar's value.

Inflation Coverage: endorsement to a homeowner's policy that automatically adjusts the amount of insurance to compensate for inflationary rises in the home's value. This type of coverage does not adjust for increases in the home's value due to improvements.

Inquiry: a credit report request. Each time a credit application is completed or more credit is requested counts as an inquiry. A large number of inquiries on a credit report can sometimes make a credit score lower.

Interest: a fee charged for the use of borrowing money.

Interest Rate: the amount of interest charged on a monthly loan payment, expressed as a percentage.

Insurance: protection against a specific loss, such as fire, wind etc., over a period of time that is secured by the payment of a regularly scheduled premium.

J

Joint Tenancy (with Rights of Survivorship): two or more owners share equal ownership and rights to the property. If a joint owner dies, his or her share of the property passes to the other owners, without probate. In joint tenancy, ownership of the property cannot be willed to someone who is not a joint owner.

Judgment: a legal decision; when requiring debt repayment, a judgment may include a property lien that secures the creditor's claim by providing a collateral source.

Jumbo Loan: or non-conforming loan, is a loan that exceeds Fannie Mae's and Freddie Mac's loan limits. Freddie Mac and Fannie Mae loans are referred to as conforming loans.

K

L

Late Payment Charges: the penalty the homeowner must pay when a mortgage payment is made after the due date grace period.

Lease: a written agreement between a property owner and a tenant (resident) that stipulates the payment and conditions under which the tenant may occupy a home or apartment and states a specified period of time.

Lease Purchase (Lease Option): assists low to moderate income homebuyers in purchasing a home by allowing them to lease a home with an option to buy; the rent payment is made up of the monthly rental payment plus an additional amount that is credited to an account for use as a down payment.

Lender: A term referring to an person or company that makes loans for real estate purchases. Sometimes referred to as a loan officer or lender.

Lender Option Commitments: an agreement giving a lender the option to deliver loans or securities by a certain date at agreed upon terms.

Liabilities: a person's financial obligations such as long-term / short-term debt, and other financial obligations to be paid.

Liability Insurance: insurance coverage that protects against claims alleging a property owner's negligence or action resulted in bodily injury or damage to another person. It is normally included in homeowner's insurance policies.

Lien: a legal claim against property that must be satisfied when the property is sold. A claim of money against a property, wherein the value of the property is used as security in repayment of a debt. Examples include a mechanic's lien, which might be for the unpaid cost of building supplies, or a tax lien for unpaid property taxes. A lien is a defect on the title and needs to be settled before transfer of ownership. A lien release is a written report of the settlement of a lien and is recorded in the public record as evidence of payment.

Lien Waiver: A document that releases a consumer (home-owner) from any further obligation for payment of a debt once it has been paid in full. Lien waivers typically are used by home-owners who hire a contractor to provide work and materials to prevent any subcontractors or suppliers of materials from filing a lien against the homeowner for nonpayment.

Life Cap: a limit on the range interest rates can increase or decrease over the life of an adjustable-rate mortgage (ARM).

Line of Credit: an agreement by a financial institution such as a bank to extend credit up to a certain amount for a certain time to a specified borrower.

Liquid Asset: a cash asset or an asset that is easily converted into cash.

Listing Agreement: a contract between a seller and a real estate professional to market and sell a home. A listing agreement obligates the real estate professional (or his or her agent) to seek qualified buyers, report all purchase offers and help negotiate the highest possible price and most favorable terms for the property seller.

Loan: money borrowed that is usually repaid with interest.

Loan Acceleration: an acceleration clause in a loan document is a statement in a mortgage that gives the lender the right to demand payment of the entire outstanding balance if a monthly payment is missed.

Loan Fraud: purposely giving incorrect information on a loan application in order to better qualify for a loan; may result in civil liability or criminal penalties.

Loan Officer: a representative of a lending or mortgage company who is responsible for soliciting homebuyers, qualifying and processing of loans. They may also be called lender, loan representative, account executive or loan rep.

Loan Origination Fee: a charge by the lender to cover the administrative costs of making the mortgage. This charge is paid at the closing and varies with the lender and type of loan. A loan origination fee of 1 to 2 percent of the mortgage amount is common.

Loan Servicer: the company that collects monthly mortgage payments and disperses property taxes and insurance payments. Loan servicers also monitor nonperforming loans, contact delinquent borrowers, and notify insurers and investors of potential problems. Loan servicers may be the lender or a specialized company that just handles loan servicing under contract with the lender or the investor who owns the loan.

Loan to Value (LTV) Ratio: a percentage calculated by dividing the amount borrowed by the price or appraised value of the home to be purchased; the higher the LTV, the less cash a borrower is required to pay as down payment.

Lock-In: since interest rates can change frequently, many lenders offer an interest rate lock-in that guarantees a specific interest rate if the loan is closed within a specific time.

Lock-in Period: the length of time that the lender has guaranteed a specific interest rate to a borrower.

Loss Mitigation: a process to avoid foreclosure; the lender tries to help a borrower who has been unable to make loan payments and is in danger of defaulting on his or her loan

M

Mandatory Delivery Commitment: an agreement that a lender will deliver loans or securities by a certain date at agreed-upon terms.

Margin: the number of percentage points the lender adds to the index rate to calculate the ARM interest rate at each adjustment.

Market Value: the amount a willing buyer would pay a willing seller for a home. An appraised value is an estimate of the current fair market value.

Maturity: the date when the principal balance of a loan becomes due and payable.

Median Price: the price of the house that falls in the middle of the total number of homes for sale in that area.

Medium Term Notes: unsecured general obligations of Fannie Mae with maturities of one day or more and with principal and interest payable in U.S. dollars.

Merged Credit Report: raw data pulled from two or more of the major credit-reporting firms.

Mitigation: term usually used to refer to various changes or improvements made in a home; for instance, to reduce the average level of radon.

Modification: when a lender agrees to modify the terms of a mortgage without refinancing the loan.

Mortgage: a lien on the property that secures the Promise to repay a loan. A security agreement between the lender and the buyer in which the property is collateral for the loan. The mortgage gives the lender the right to collect payment on the loan and to foreclose if the loan obligations are not met.

Mortgage Acceleration Clause: a clause allowing a lender, under certain circumstances, demand the entire balance of a loan is repaid in a lump sum. The acceleration clause is usually triggered if the home is sold, title to the property is changed, the loan is refinanced or the borrower defaults on a scheduled payment.

Mortgage-Backed Security (MBS): a Fannie Mae security that represents an undivided interest in a group of mortgages. Principal and interest payments from the individual mortgage loans are grouped and paid out to the MBS holders.

Mortgage Banker: a company that originates loans and resells them to secondary mortgage lenders like Fannie Mae or Freddie Mac.

Mortgage Broker: a firm that originates and processes loans for a number of lenders.

Mortgage Life and Disability Insurance: term life insurance bought by borrowers to pay off a mortgage in the event of death or make monthly payments in the case of disability. The amount of coverage decreases as the principal balance declines. There are many different terms of coverage determining amounts of payments and when payments begin and end.

Mortgage Insurance: a policy that protects lenders against some or most of the losses that can occur when a borrower defaults on a mortgage loan; mortgage insurance is required primarily for borrowers with a down payment of less than 20% of the home's purchase price. Insurance purchased by the buyer to protect the lender in the event of default. Typically purchased for loans with less than 20 percent down payment. The cost of mortgage insurance is usually added to the monthly payment. Mortgage insurance is maintained on conventional loans until the outstanding amount of the loan is less than 80 percent of the value of the house or for a set period of time (7 years is common). Mortgage insurance also is available through a government agency, such as the Federal Housing Administration (FHA) or through companies (Private Mortgage Insurance or PMI).

Mortgage Insurance Premium (MIP): a monthly payment -usually part of the mortgage payment - paid by a borrower for mortgage insurance.

Mortgage Interest Deduction: the interest cost of a mortgage, which is a tax - deductible expense. The interest reduces the taxable income of taxpayers.

Mortgage Modification: a loss mitigation option that allows a borrower to refinance and/or extend the term of the mortgage loan and thus reduce the monthly payments.

Mortgage Note: a legal document obligating a borrower to repay a loan at a stated interest rate during a specified period; the agreement is secured by a mortgage that is recorded in the public records along with the deed.

Mortgage Qualifying Ratio: Used to calculate the maximum amount of funds that an individual traditionally may be able to afford. A typical mortgage qualifying ratio is 28: 36.

Mortgage Score: a score based on a combination of information about the borrower that is obtained from the loan application, the credit report, and property value information. The score is a comprehensive analysis of the borrower's ability to repay a mortgage loan and manage credit.

Mortgagee: the lender in a mortgage agreement. Mortgagor - The borrower in a mortgage agreement.

Mortgagor: the borrower in a mortgage agreement

Multifamily Housing: a building with more than four residential rental units.

Multiple Listing Service (MLS): within the Metro Columbus area, Realtors submit listings and agree to attempt to sell all properties in the MLS. The MLS is a service of the local Columbus Board of Realtors®. The local MLS has a protocol for updating listings and sharing commissions. The MLS offers the advantage of more timely information, availability, and access to houses and other types of property on the market.

N

National Credit Repositories: currently, there are three companies that maintain national credit - reporting databases. These are Equifax, Experian, and Trans Union, referred to as Credit Bureaus.

Negative Amortization: amortization means that monthly payments are large enough to pay the interest and reduce the principal on your mortgage. Negative amortization occurs when the monthly payments do not cover all of the interest cost. The interest cost that isn't covered is added to the unpaid principal balance. This means that even after making many payments, you could owe more than you did at the beginning of the loan.

Negative amortization can occur when an ARM has a payment cap that results in monthly payments not high enough to cover the interest due.

Net Income: Your take-home pay, the amount of money that you receive in your paycheck after taxes and deductions.

No Cash Out Refinance: a refinance of an existing loan only for the amount remaining on the mortgage. The borrower does not get any cash against the equity of the home. Also called a "rate and term refinance."

No Cost Loan: there are many variations of a no cost loan. Generally, it is a loan that does not charge for items such as title insurance, escrow fees, settlement fees, appraisal, recording fees or notary fees. It may also offer no points. This lessens the need for upfront cash during the buying process however no cost loans have a higher interest rate.

Nonperforming Asset: an asset such as a mortgage that is not currently accruing interest or which interest is not being paid.

Note: a legal document obligating a borrower to repay a mortgage loan at a stated interest rate over a specified period of time.

Note Rate: the interest rate stated on a mortgage note.

Notice of Default: a formal written notice to a borrower that there is a default on a loan and that legal action is possible.

Non-Conforming loan: is a loan that exceeds Fannie Mae's and Freddie Mac's loan limits. Freddie Mac and Fannie Mae loans are referred to as conforming loans.

Notary Public: a person who serves as a public official and certifies the authenticity of required signatures on a document by signing and stamping the document.

O

Offer: indication by a potential buyer of a willingness to purchase a home at a specific price; generally put forth in writing.

Original Principal Balance: the total principal owed on a mortgage prior to any payments being made.

Origination: the process of preparing, submitting, and evaluating a loan application; generally includes a credit check, verification of employment, and a property appraisal.

Origination Fee: the charge for originating a loan; is usually calculated in the form of points and paid at closing. One point equals one percent of the loan amount. On a conventional loan, the loan origination fee is the number of points a borrower pays.

Owner Financing: a home purchase where the seller provides all or part of the financing, acting as a lender.

Ownership: ownership is documented by the deed to a property. The type or form of ownership is important if there is a change in the status of the owners or if the property changes ownership.

Owner's Policy: the insurance policy that protects the buyer from title defects.

P

PITI: Principal, Interest, Taxes, and Insurance: the four elements of a monthly mortgage payment; payments of principal and interest go directly towards repaying the loan while the portion that covers taxes and insurance (homeowner's and mortgage, if applicable) goes into an escrow account to cover the fees when they are due.

PITI Reserves: a cash amount that a borrower must have on hand after making a down payment and paying all closing costs for the purchase of a home. The principal, interest, taxes, and insurance (PITI) reserves must equal the amount that the borrower would have to pay for PITI for a predefined number of months.

PMI: Private Mortgage Insurance; privately-owned companies that offer standard and special affordable mortgage insurance programs for qualified borrowers with down payments of less than 20% of a purchase price.

Partial Payment: a payment that is less than the total amount owed on a monthly mortgage payment. Normally, lenders do not accept partial payments. The lender may make exceptions during times of difficulty. Contact your lender prior to the due date if a partial payment is needed.

Payment Cap: a limit on how much an ARM's payment may increase, regardless of how much the interest rate increases.

Payment Change Date: the date when a new monthly payment amount takes effect on an adjustable-rate mortgage (ARM) or a graduated-payment mortgage (GPM). Generally, the payment change date occurs in the month immediately after the interest rate adjustment date.

Payment Due Date: Contract language specifying when payments are due on money borrowed. The due date is always indicated and means that the payment must be received on or before the specified date. Grace periods prior to assessing a late fee or additional interest do not eliminate the responsibility of making payments on time.

Perils: for homeowner's insurance, an event that can damage the property. Homeowner's insurance may cover the property for a wide variety of perils caused by accidents, nature, or people.

Personal Property: any property that is not real property or attached to real property. For example furniture is not attached however a new light fixture would be considered attached and part of the real property.

Planned Unit Development (PUD): a development that is planned, and constructed as one entity. Generally, there are common features in the homes or lots governed by covenants attached to the deed. Most planned developments have common land and facilities owned and managed by the owner's or neighborhood association. Homeowners usually are required to participate in the association via a payment of annual dues.

Points: a point is equal to one percent of the principal amount of your mortgage. For example, if you get a mortgage for $95,000, one point means you pay $950 to the lender. Lenders frequently charge points in both fixed-rate and adjustable-rate mortgages in order to increase the yield on the mortgage and to cover loan closing costs. These points usually are collected at closing and may be paid by the borrower or the home seller, or may be split between them.

Power of Attorney: a legal document that authorizes another person to act on your behalf. A power of attorney can grant complete authority or can be limited to certain acts or certain periods of time or both.

Pre-Approval: a lender commits to lend to a potential borrower a fixed loan amount based on a completed loan application, credit reports, debt, savings and has been reviewed by an underwriter. The commitment remains as long as the borrower still meets the qualification requirements at the time of purchase. This does not guaranty a loan until the property has passed inspections underwriting guidelines.

Predatory Lending: abusive lending practices that include a mortgage loan to someone who does not have the ability to repay. It also pertains to repeated refinancing of a loan charging high interest and fees each time.

Predictive Variables: The variables that are part of the formula comprising elements of a credit-scoring model. These variables are used to predict a borrower's future credit performance.

Preferred Stock: stock that takes priority over common stock with regard to dividends and liquidation rights. Preferred stockholders typically have no voting rights.

Pre-foreclosure Sale: a procedure in which the borrower is allowed to sell a property for an amount less than what is owed on it to avoid a foreclosure. This sale fully satisfies the borrower's debt.

Prepayment: any amount paid to reduce the principal balance of a loan before the due date or payment in full of a mortgage. This can occur with the sale of the property, the pay off the loan in full, or a foreclosure. In each case, full payment occurs before the loan has been fully amortized.

Prepayment Penalty: a provision in some loans that charge a fee to a borrower who pays off a loan before it is due.

Pre-Foreclosure sale: allows a defaulting borrower to sell the mortgaged property to satisfy the loan and avoid foreclosure.

Pre-Qualify: a lender informally determines the maximum amount an individual is eligible to borrow. This is not a guaranty of a loan.

Premium: an amount paid on a regular schedule by a policy-holder that maintains insurance coverage.

Prepayment: payment of the mortgage loan before the scheduled due date; may be Subject to a prepayment penalty.

Prepayment Penalty: a fee charged to a homeowner who pays one or more monthly payments before the due date. It can also apply to principal reduction payments.

Prepayment Penalty Mortgage (PPM): a type of mortgage that requires the borrower to pay a penalty for prepayment, partial payment of principal or for repaying the entire loan within a certain time period. A partial payment is generally defined as an amount exceeding 20% of the original principal balance.

Price Range: the high and low amount a buyer is willing to pay for a home.

Prime Rate: the interest rate that banks charge to preferred customers. Changes in the prime rate are publicized in the business media. Prime rate can be used as the basis for adjustable rate mortgages (ARMs) or home equity lines of credit. The prime rate also affects the current interest rates being offered at a particular point in time on fixed mortgages. Changes in the prime rate do not affect the interest on a fixed mortgage.

Principal: the amount of money borrowed to buy a house or the amount of the loan that has not been paid back to the lender. This does not include the interest paid to borrow that money. The principal balance is the amount owed on a loan at any given time. It is the original loan amount minus the total repayments of principal made.

Principal, Interest, Taxes, and Insurance (PITI): the four elements of a monthly mortgage payment; payments of principal and interest go directly towards repaying the loan while the portion that covers taxes and insurance (homeowner's and mortgage, if applicable) goes into an escrow account to cover the fees when they are due.

Private Mortgage Insurance (PMI): insurance purchased by a buyer to protect the lender in the event of default. The cost of mortgage insurance is usually added to the monthly payment. Mortgage insurance is generally maintained until over 20 Percent of the outstanding amount of the loan is paid or for a set period of time, seven years is normal. Mortgage insurance may be available through a government agency, such as the Federal Housing Administration (FHA) or the Veterans Administration (VA), or through private mortgage insurance companies (PMI).

Promissory Note: a written promise to repay a specified amount over a specified period of time.

Property (Fixture and Non-Fixture): in a real estate contract, the property is the land within the legally described boundaries and all permanent structures and fixtures. Ownership of the property confers the legal right to use the property as allowed within the law and within the restrictions of zoning or easements. Fixture property refers to those items permanently attached to the structure, such as carpeting or a ceiling fan, which transfers with the property.

Property Tax: a tax charged by local government and used to fund municipal services such as schools, police, or street maintenance. The amount of property tax is determined locally by a formula, usually based on a percent per $1,000 of assessed value of the property.

Property Tax Deduction: the U.S. tax code allows homeowners to deduct the amount they have paid in property taxes from there total income.

Public Record Information: Court records of events that are a matter of public interest such as credit, bankruptcy, foreclosure and tax liens. The presence of public record information on a credit report is regarded negatively by creditors.

Punch List: a list of items that have not been completed at the time of the final walk through of a newly constructed home.

Purchase Offer: A detailed, written document that makes an offer to purchase a property, and that may be amended several times in the process of negotiations. When signed by all parties involved in the sale, the purchase offer becomes a legally binding contract, sometimes called the Sales Contract.

Q

Qualifying Ratios: guidelines utilized by lenders to determine how much money a homebuyer is qualified to borrow. Lending guidelines typically include a maximum housing expense to income ratio and a maximum monthly expense to income ratio.

Quitclaim Deed: a deed transferring ownership of a property but does not make any guarantee of clear title.

R

RESPA: Real Estate Settlement Procedures Act; a law protecting consumers from abuses during the residential real estate purchase and loan process by requiring lenders to disclose all settlement costs, practices, and relationships

Radon: a radioactive gas found in some homes that, if occurring in strong enough concentrations, can cause health problems.

Rate Cap: a limit on an ARM on how much the interest rate or mortgage payment may change. Rate caps limit how much the interest rates can rise or fall on the adjustment dates and over the life of the loan.

Rate Lock: a commitment by a lender to a borrower guaranteeing a specific interest rate over a period of time at a set cost.

Real Estate Agent: an individual who is licensed to negotiate and arrange real estate sales; works for a real estate broker.

Real Estate Mortgage Investment Conduit (REMIC): a security representing an interest in a trust having multiple classes of securities. The securities of each class entitle investors to cash payments structured differently from the payments on the underlying mortgages.

Real Estate Property Tax Deduction: a tax deductible expense reducing a taxpayer's taxable income.

Real Estate Settlement Procedures Act (RESPA): a law protecting consumers from abuses during the residential real estate purchase and loan process by requiring lenders to disclose all settlement costs, practices, and relationships

Real Property: land, including all the natural resources and permanent buildings on it.

REALTOR®: a real estate agent or broker who is a member of the NATIONAL ASSOCIATION OF REALTORS, and its local and state associations. **Recorder:** the public official who keeps records of transactions concerning real property. Sometimes known as a "Registrar of Deeds" or "County Clerk."

Recording: the recording in a registrar's office of an executed legal document. These include deeds, mortgages, satisfaction of a mortgage, or an extension of a mortgage making it a part of the public record.

Recording Fees: charges for recording a deed with the appropriate government agency.

Refinancing: paying off one loan by obtaining another; refinancing is generally done to secure better loan terms (like a lower interest rate).

Rehabilitation Mortgage: a mortgage that covers the costs of rehabilitating (repairing or Improving) a property; some rehabilitation mortgages - like the FHA's 203(k) - allow a borrower to roll the costs of rehabilitation and home purchase into one mortgage loan.

Reinstatement Period: a phase of the foreclosure process where the homeowner has an opportunity to stop the foreclosure by paying money that is owed to the lender.

Remaining Balance: the amount of principal that has not yet been repaid.

Remaining Term: the original amortization term minus the number of payments that have been applied.

Repayment plan: an agreement between a lender and a delinquent borrower where the borrower agrees to make additional payments to pay down past due amounts while making regularly scheduled payments.

Return On Average Common Equity: net income available to common stockholders, as a percentage of average common stockholder equity.

Reverse Mortgage (HECM): the reverse mortgage is used by senior homeowners age 62 and older to convert the equity in their home into monthly streams of income and/or a line of credit to be repaid when they no longer occupy the home. A lending institution such as a mortgage lender, bank, credit union or savings and loan association funds the FHA insured loan, commonly known as HECM.

Right of First Refusal: a provision in an agreement that requires the owner of a property to give one party an opportunity to purchase or lease a property before it is offered for sale or lease to others.

S

Sale Leaseback: when a seller deeds property to a buyer for a payment, and the buyer simultaneously leases the property back to the seller.

Second Mortgage: an additional mortgage on property. In case of a default the first mortgage must be paid before the second mortgage. Second loans are more risky for the lender and usually carry a higher interest rate.

Secondary Mortgage Market: the buying and selling of mortgage loans. Investors purchase residential mortgages originated by lenders, which in turn provides the lenders with capital for additional lending.

Secured Loan: a loan backed by collateral such as property.

Security: the property that will be pledged as collateral for a loan.

Seller Carry Back/Seller Financing: an agreement where the owner of a property provides second mortgage financing. These are often combined with an assumed mortgage instead of a portion of the seller's equity.

Serious Delinquency: a mortgage that is 90 days or more past due.

Servicer: a business that collects mortgage payments from borrowers and manages the borrower's escrow accounts.

Servicing: the collection of mortgage payments from borrowers and related responsibilities of a loan servicer.

Setback: the distance between a property line and the area where building can take place. Setbacks are used to assure space between buildings and from roads for a many of purposes including drainage and utilities.

Settlement: another name for closing.

Settlement Statement: a document required by the Real Estate Settlement Procedures Act (RESPA). It is an itemized statement of services and charges relating to the closing of a property transfer. The buyer has the right to examine the settlement statement 1 day before the closing. This is called the HUD 1 Settlement Statement.

Stockholders' Equity: the sum of proceeds from the issuance of stock and retained earnings less amounts paid to repurchase common shares.

Stripped MBS (SMBS): securities created by "stripping" or separating the principal and interest payments from the underlying pool of mortgages into two classes of securities, with each receiving a different proportion of the principal and interest payments.

Sub-Prime Loan: "B" Loan or "B" paper with FICO scores from 620 - 659. "C" Loan or "C" Paper with FICO scores typically from 580 to 619. An industry term to used to describe loans with less stringent lending and underwriting terms and conditions. Due to the higher risk, sub-prime loans charge higher interest rates and fees.

Subordinate: to place in a rank of lesser importance or to make one claim secondary to another.

Survey: a property diagram that indicates legal boundaries, easements, encroachments, rights of way, improvement locations, etc. Surveys are conducted by licensed surveyors and are normally required by the lender in order to confirm that the property boundaries and features such as buildings, and easements are correctly described in the legal description of the property.

Sweat Equity: using labor to build or improve a property as part of the down payment

T

Third Party Origination: a process by which a lender uses another party to completely or partially originate, process, underwrite, close, fund, or package the mortgages it plans to deliver to the secondary mortgage market.

Terms: The period of time and the interest rate agreed upon by the lender and the borrower to repay a loan.

Title: a legal document establishing the right of ownership and is recorded to make it part of the public record. Also known as a Deed.

Title 1: an FHA-insured loan that allows a borrower to make non-luxury improvements (like renovations or repairs) to their home; Title I loans less than $7,500 don't require a property lien.

Title Company: a company that specializes in examining and insuring titles to real estate.

Title Defect: an outstanding claim on a property that limits the ability to sell the property. Also referred to as a cloud on the title.

Title Insurance: insurance that protects the lender against any claims that arise from arguments about ownership of the property; also available for homebuyers. An insurance policy guaranteeing the accuracy of a title search protecting against errors. Most lenders require the buyer to purchase title insurance protecting the lender against loss in the event of a title defect. This charge is included in the closing costs. A policy that protects the buyer from title defects is known as an owner's policy and requires an additional charge.

Title Search: a check of public records to be sure that the seller is the recognized owner of the real estate and that there are no unsettled liens or other claims against the property.

Transfer Agent: a bank or trust company charged with keeping a record of a company's stockholders and canceling and issuing certificates as shares are bought and sold.

Transfer of Ownership: any means by which ownership of a property changes hands. These include purchase of a property, assumption of mortgage debt, exchange of possession of a property via a land sales contract or any other land trust device.

Transfer Taxes: State and local taxes charged for the transfer of real estate. Usually equal to a percentage of the sales price.

Treasury Index: can be used as the basis for adjustable rate mortgages (ARMs) It is based on the results of auctions that the U.S. Treasury holds for its Treasury bills and securities.

Truth-in-Lending: a federal law obligating a lender to give full written disclosure of all fees, terms, and conditions associated with the loan initial period and then adjusts to another rate that lasts for the term of the loan.

Two Step Mortgage: an adjustable-rate mortgage (ARM) that has one interest rate for the first five to seven years of its term and a different interest rate for the remainder of the term.

Trustee: a person who holds or controls property for the benefit of another.

U

Underwriting: the process of analyzing a loan application to determine the amount of risk involved in making the loan; it includes a review of the potential borrower's credit history and a judgment of the property value.

Up Front Charges: the fees charged to homeowners by the lender at the time of closing a mortgage loan. This includes points, broker's fees, insurance, and other charges.

V

VA (Department of Veterans Affairs): a federal agency, which guarantees loans made to veterans; similar to mortgage insurance, a loan guarantee protects lenders against loss that may result from a borrower default.

VA Mortgage: a mortgage guaranteed by the Department of Veterans Affairs (VA).

Variable Expenses: Costs or payments that may vary from month to month, for example, gasoline or food.

Variance: a special exemption of a zoning law to allow the property to be used in a manner different from an existing law.

Vested: a point in time when you may withdraw funds from an investment account, such as a retirement account, without penalty.

W

Walk Through: the final inspection of a property being sold by the buyer to confirm that any contingencies specified in the purchase agreement such as repairs have been completed, fixture and non-fixture property is in place and confirm the electrical, mechanical, and plumbing systems are in working order.

Warranty Deed: a legal document that includes the guarantee the seller is the true owner of the property, has the right to sell the property and there are no claims against the property.

X

Y

Z

Zoning: local laws established to control the uses of land within a particular area. Zoning laws are used to separate residential land from areas of non-residential use, such as industry or businesses. Zoning ordinances include many provisions governing such things as type of structure, setbacks, lot size, and uses of a building.

————————————

Source: Information provided by the Department of Housing and Urban Development.

www.ingramcontent.com/pod-product-compliance
Lightning Source LLC
Chambersburg PA
CBHW061608220326
41598CB00024BC/3500